THE CREEK

SHIRLEE P. NEWMAN

THE CREEK

Franklin Watts   A Division of Grolier Publishing
New York   London   Hong Kong   Sydney   Danbury, Connecticut
A First Book

For Haley

FRONTIS: THIS HANDMADE CLAY POT SHOWS THE ANCIENT CREEK
PEOPLE IN THE SOUTHEASTERN UNITED STATES.

Map by
Cover photograph ©: Ben Klaffke
Photographs ©: Ben Klaffke: pp. 3, 9, 11, 12, 15 (both photos), 17, 20, 23 right,
25, 42, 50, 53, 56; Bettmann Archive: p. 36; Newberry Library: p. 54; North Wind
Picture Archives: pp. 28, 31; Oklahoma Historical Society, Archives & Manuscripts
Division: pp. 19, 34, 36, 46; Gilder Lehrman Collection, "The Papers of Henry
Knox," on deposit at The Pierpont Morgan Library, New York: p. 33; Western
History Collections, University of Oklahoma Library, J. W. Morris Collection: pp.
23 left, 45; Woolaroc Museum, Battlesville, OK: p. 41.

Library of Congress Cataloging-in-Publication Data
Newman, Shirlee P.
The Creek / by Shirlee P. Newman.
p. cm. — (A First book)
Includes bibliographical references and index.
Summary: Discusses the history, culture, and daily life of the Creek Indians.
ISBN 0–531–20236–4 (lib. bdg.) — ISBN 0–531–15809–8 (pbk.)
1. Creek Indians—Juvenile literature. [1. Creek Indians. 2. Indians of North
America.] I. Title. II. Series.
E99.C9N49 1996
975'.004973—dc20   95-49036 CIP AC

CONTENTS

THE MASTER OF BREATHS

Dense fog covered the earth when the Master of Breaths created it. The fog clung to trees and hung low over water and land. People heard animals but could not see them or each other. Then one person snorted like a bear. Another bellowed like an alligator. Someone else chirped like a bird. At last a breeze blew, gently at first, then stronger until it became so powerful it blew away the fog.

"My clan will be as powerful as that," a woman said. "I shall call it the Wind Clan."

A beaver swam by with two sticks in its mouth. "My clan will be as diligent as that," a second woman said. "I shall call it the Beaver Clan."

A tiny green shoot pushed up through the ground. "My clan will start small," a third woman said. "But we will grow fast and flourish and nourish each other. I shall call my clan the Sweet Potato Clan."

Other people did the same. Thus each *clan* of the Creek Indians got its name.

The Creek People ➡ The Creeks' ancestors—the first people who lived in the southeastern United States—were called the Mississippians. They lived there for hundreds of years and built great earthen mounds that still stand. Temples that once stood on top of some of the mounds probably honored their gods. Other mounds were burial places. Artifacts found in those mounds—pots, dishes, vases, and tools—were decorated with carvings that show respect for their chiefs, who were also religious leaders.

The Mississippian culture had declined by the 1500s, when the first Spanish explorers came to this part of what they called the New World. The Spanish found several groups of people who lived in distant villages but stayed in contact with each other for protection. The first Native Americans that English traders met when they came to the Southeast lived near a creek, so the traders called all Native Americans in the region Creeks. Actually, there were several tribes with different names, some of them Muscogee. Later they all came to be known as Muscogee or Creek, as they are known today.

The explorers met Muscogee people who were tall, well fed, and strong. But not for long. The Spaniards brought deadly diseases to which native people were not immune. Thousands died and whole villages were wiped out.

OKLAHOMA, WHERE MOST CREEK LIVE TODAY, IS DIFFERENT FROM THEIR HOME IN THE SOUTHEASTERN UNITED STATES, BUT ITS SUNSETS ARE JUST AS BEAUTIFUL.

In the 1600s, villages in which hundreds had died combined with others. There were fifty towns joined together in the powerful Creek Confederacy, or alliance. Spain, Britain, and France all tried to take control of the region. Creeks became caught up in their struggle. After years of conflict, they were defeated by the Americans in the Creek War of 1813–1814. They were forced to give up most of their land and were later moved to Indian Territory (now Oklahoma).

About fifty thousand Native Americans called Muscogees or Creeks live in the United States today, most in Oklahoma, some in southern Alabama.

HOW THE CREEK LIVED

Creek people did not need to move around, as did many other Native Americans. They combined agriculture with hunting and gathering. In the Southeast winters are mild and summers long. Edible plants grew wild. Animals roamed the woodlands. Rivers and streams teemed with fish. The Creek fished with floating traps, lines made of plant fibers, and bone hooks. In shallow places Creek men sprinkled the water with powdered root that stunned the fish so they floated to the top and could be scooped up.

Before European traders arrived, Creek men killed deer only for food and clothing. They also used the bones as tools. Hunters would paint their cheeks with red ochre (dirt with iron deposits in it) because they believed it sharpened their vision. They sang special songs that drew deer close and made them easier to kill. Men also hunted for bears, squirrels, birds, and rabbits. They used wooden spears, bows and arrows, and cane blowguns. After the arrival of

SOME CREEK STILL HUNT WITH BOW AND ARROW,
AS THEIR ANCESTORS DID.

THIS CREEK WOMAN SHOWS HER GRANDCHILDREN
HOW TO WEAVE A TRADITIONAL BASKET.

European explorers, Creek men hunted deer for trade as well as food.

Women planted, weeded, and picked crops, such as corn, beans, squash, and pumpkins. They also gathered wild plants, cared for children, wove baskets and mats, made clothing and clay pots, and prepared and cooked food. In winter a pot of stew bubbled over the fire and a bowl of *sofky* (cornmeal broth) stood near the door for guests. Some women were *midwives* and *herbalists*. Some sat in council, or assembly, with the men.

Homes and Villages ➡ Many families had summer and winter homes. Summer homes—thatched roofs held up by poles—were cool and breezy. Winter homes, with mud walls and fires inside, were snug and warm. The only openings in a winter home were a smoke hole in the roof and a small door. Summer and winter homes were near each other. Parents, children, grandchildren, grandparents, and perhaps a future son-in-law or an orphan or two all lived together.

Shared growing fields surrounded Creek *italwas*, or towns. Ceremonial buildings stood on one side of the town square. One of the most important buildings was the *chakofa*, used for winter council meetings. This tall, round structure had mud walls supported by vertical wooden posts. The cone-shaped roof, made of tree bark or thatch, had no smoke hole. Instead, special dry wood with its bark stripped off was used in the inside fire to lessen smoke.

Creek settlements occupied the flatlands of the Southeast. Much of this area is now Georgia and Alabama. Towns were designated either as white towns, for peace ceremonies, or Chiloki (or red) towns, for war ceremonies. The Upper Creeks, those to the north, were mostly from Muscogee tribes. Later they became known as *Red Sticks*. They thought the red-painted sticks their fighters carried would protect them. The Lower Creeks were mostly from the Hitchiti and Alabama tribes.

Games ➡ Opposite the ceremonial buildings in town was an open space for festivals and games. Young men played a noisy, exciting ball game called stickball, or "Little Brother to War." The French called this game *la crosse*. Other tribes also played versions of stickball. The game was so rough-and-tumble that *shamans*, or medicine men, circled the field to take care of scratches, bruises, and broken bones.

Stickball players used two sticks with woven nets or leather loops at one end. They kicked, wrestled, or struck one another's sticks to capture the ball and carry or hurl it through goalposts. When rival teams

THE GAME OF STICKBALL DEMANDS SKILL, SPEED, AND COURAGE.
THE RULES ARE SIMILAR TO THOSE FOR MODERN LACROSSE.

from different italwas faced each other, hundreds of players might be on the field, their shouts mingling with cheers and jeers of spectators. The Creeks' ball courts had sloping sides so spectators could easily follow the action.

Younger boys played a game called chunkey, for fun and as practice for accurate spear throwing. One player shoved a stone disk so that it rolled down the field. Players chased it with a long stick, curved at one end, and hurled their sticks to where they expected the disk to stop. Chunkey was a lot tamer than stickball. Sometimes the whole family played chunkey together.

Family Life ➡ Families were important to Creek people. Cousins, uncles, aunts, and grandparents belonged to the same clan and often lived in the same town, close to each other. Sometimes they placed a *totem* near their homes to indicate their particular clan. Members of the Deer Clan might have a deer's skull attached to the top of their totem. The Sweet Potato Clan might put a sweet potato on top. Certain men and women, often elders, from various clans who lived in the town, were selected to advise the *mico*, who governed it. Connections between clans were also important to the Creek Confederacy. Clan members kept distant towns in contact with each other.

THE ARCHWAY OVER THE WALK TO THIS MAN'S HOUSE
IS A TOTEM. IT DISPLAYS ANCIENT CLAN SYMBOLS OF
THE EAGLE AND ALLIGATOR.

It was *taboo* for members of the same clan to marry. If a young man of another clan wished to marry a girl, he sent her a gift. Before Europeans arrived, gifts were usually food, furs, or bear oil. After European traders came, trade goods such as blankets, beads, and cloth also became popular gifts. If the women in the clan thought the young man would be a good husband and the girl accepted his proposal, the couple was considered temporarily married. The young man came to live in the girl's home and helped her in the fields. If the couple still wished to marry after a year passed, a wedding was held. They could divorce only at *Poskita*, the Green Corn Festival, but if they had children they seldom did so.

Mothers, aunts (specifically sisters of mothers), and grandmothers taught girls. Uncles (specifically brothers of mothers) taught boys. Girls learned to cook, weave baskets and cloth, sew, and sing songs when searching for edible plants. Uncles taught boys to hunt, fish, and build houses and boats. Parents loved their children but punished them when they were naughty. One observer wrote that older children might be scratched when they misbehaved "to let out the evil that caused the misbehavior," but this might not be true.

THIS CREEK WOMAN IN 1926 WEARS A VARIETY
OF TRADITIONAL CLOTHING.

IMAGINATIVE PAINTING OF A CREEK SHAMAN, OR MICO, BY
ANTHONY MITCHELL, A FULL-BLOODED CREEK-SEMINOLE

Clothing ➤ Because of the Southeast's mild winter and hot, long summer, Creeks wore little clothing. Men wore deerskin *breechcloths.* Women wore skirts made of deerskin or of cloth woven from rabbit hair, *Spanish moss,* or cotton. Both men and women sometimes wore grass shawls over one shoulder. In summer, children wore no clothes at all until they were about twelve.

Men often painted their bodies or tattooed their skin by pricking it with porcupine needles dipped in plant dyes. Warriors tattooed themselves with special designs that showed their courage. Women's designs indicated their status, clan, or husbands' position in the tribe. The mico painted his face half red and half black for special occasions. He circled one eye with white paint and the other with black for everyday appearances.

CUSTOMS AND BELIEFS

Poskita ➤ Corn could be dried and stored, popped, roasted, and pounded into flour. It was so important the Creeks named a goddess after it. The Corn Goddess washed her feet in the stream, the corn legend says. When she dried her feet, corn sprouted from her toes. The Green Corn Festival was, and still is, extremely important to Creeks. The festival itself lasted four to eight days in July or August, but preparations took several weeks. Everything had to be fresh and clean to please the Corn Goddess.

Creek men scrubbed public buildings, then swept the town square and covered it with white sand. Women cleaned their homes and decorated them with flowers and leafy boughs. They wove new mats, sewed new clothes, made new pots, and threw away the old. Men drank a special tea that made them

CREEK WOMEN IN 1910 GRIND CORN WITH A MORTAR AND PESTLE.
TRADITIONAL BLUE CORN CAKES ARE STILL A FAVORITE.

vomit before the festival began, because they thought vomiting purified them. To atone for any wrongdoing the previous year, they fasted (went without food) and remained in the square until the festival's end. They danced and sang to thank the Corn Goddess for a bountiful harvest and to pray for a good harvest the next year.

The Shaman ➡ On the last day of Poskita, the shaman placed four logs on the ground to symbolize the four directions. As he kindled the new fire, he might chant the ancient legend about how Creeks' ancestors found sacred fire and magic herbs on their journey from the west. He might wave his arms as he told how they crossed a blood-red river, and fought a giant eagle with a wingspread so wide it darkened a whole valley when it flew overhead. He would tell how Creek ancestors climbed a singing mountain, killed a lion, and conquered people with strangely shaped heads.

After the shaman lighted the town fire, Creek women collected some of its embers to start new fires in their homes. Thus, every home and person in the town was connected, in a sense. Using the new fire, Creek women cooked freshly picked corn, sofky, and special blue corn cakes. Finally, everyone went to the

CREEK WOMEN AND CHILDREN DANCE AROUND
A SACRED POSKITA FIRE.

square and feasted, danced, sang, and played games. At the climax of the festivities, they jumped into the nearest river or creek to cleanse their bodies. The previous year's tensions were washed away and old enemies forgiven. A brand new year was begun.

Sometime during Poskita, a shaman might also chant the Creek belief that the Master of Breaths lived in the "upper world" with the sun, moon, thunder, and stars. The Master of Breaths tried to keep the "middle world," where people live, in order. The shaman would also tell of "lower world" spirits. One story describes the dreaded tie snake, who created chaos in the middle world by placing things where they didn't belong, like the plump, juicy fish a hunter found in a tree! The hunter knew fish belonged in water, not in trees, but he ate it anyway. He turned into a big ugly frog—the tie snake had done its work.

FRIENDS AND ENEMIES

Imagine what Muscogee people thought when Hernando de Soto, the Spanish explorer, came to their land in 1539 and demanded food for the five hundred men, two women, and horses, pigs, and ferocious dogs he brought with him. And imagine what Muscogees thought when the Spaniards chained Muscogee men together with iron neck collars and forced them to carry heavy loads. And what did they think when the Spaniards punished those who refused by setting the dogs on them, burning them alive, or plunging swords into their hearts?

De Soto was experienced at that sort of thing. He had been with the *conquistadors* who defeated the Incas in South America and had become wealthy on Incan gold. He thought the Muscogees might also have gold. They didn't, but they did have pearls. The Spaniards took those instead.

HERNANDO DE SOTO AND HIS MEN LANDED
AND CAMPED NEAR TAMPA BAY, FLORIDA,
THEN MARCHED NORTH.

Tuscaloosa, a famous Muscogee leader, offered to guide the Spaniards to a town where they could get more food and men to carry their loads. De Soto accepted the offer, and Tuscaloosa led him to a town near Mobile, Alabama. Tuscaloosa sent a messenger ahead, warning the town's mico to prepare his people to defend it. But their bows and arrows and wooden spears were useless against swords, guns, armor, and trampling horses. Hundreds of native people were killed, and the Spaniards burned the town to the ground.

The English, who called the Muscogee people the Creek, moved into the area in the 1600s. They established their Carolina colony, with Charles Town as its capital, in Creek territory. By the 1700s, France, England, and Spain had all set up trading posts and were competing for trade with the Creeks. Deerskins were especially valuable. Soon many Creeks felt they couldn't get along without metal pots and pans, guns, tea, cloth, and other things English traders provided. Creek hunters began killing deer just to trade. These people became known as the Nontraditionals.

Indian captives became even more valuable than deerskins. The English sold captives to *plantation* owners, who made them into slaves. In 1715 the

Yamasees, a small tribe in Carolina, killed some English settlers because the English had kidnapped Yamasee women and children and sold them into slavery. To keep peace, the English made Indian slavery illegal.

With the English in their midst, and the French and Spanish to the south, most Creeks were against taking sides in the Europeans' struggle to control the land. But some Creeks fought with the English against the Spanish in Florida and decided to stay in that area. Later, other Creeks and Africans escaping from slavery joined them. They were eventually called Seminoles, for the Spanish word *cimarrones*, meaning runaways.

Many Creek admired the English, envied their education, and learned their language. Some even thought the Master of Breaths sent the English to teach them. They gave land to the English to thank them. In 1734 a British general invited Tomochichi, mico of a town in Georgia, his wife, nephew, and six other micos to England to meet King George II. Crowds of Londoners stared at the "savages," as some people called them. Tomochichi and the others, dressed in scarlet and gold with feathers in their hair, rode to the palace in the king's royal coach.

TOMOCHICHI AS HE APPEARED IN LONDON IN 1734,
WITH HIS NEPHEW, TOOANAHOWI

The Creeks were in a tough situation when English colonists went to war to gain their independence from England. If Creeks sided with England, the colonists would become their enemies. The Creeks decided to stay neutral (not take sides) but many remained friendly with the English. In 1783, when the colonists won the war, England ceded Creek territory to the new United States. It didn't make sense to the Creeks. How could one nation give Creek land to another nation?

Other southeastern tribes were also within U.S. boundaries, so in 1803 Creek micos met with Cherokees, Choctaws, and Chickasaws. They agreed that no tribe would sell or give away land without the other tribes' consent. The plan did not work. Choctaws owed traders money and had to pay them with land. The Creeks were on their own again. Even though U.S. officials signed a treaty promising to protect Creek boundaries, whites who came to live in Creek lands were allowed to stay.

Alexander McGillivray, whose mother was a Creek of the Wind Clan and father was a Scottish settler, tried to settle the dispute. He wrote to the British in Canada, the French in Louisiana, and the Spanish in Florida, asking them to recognize the Creek Confederacy as a nation so that they would be

I Alexander McGillivray, Agent to the Creek nation of Indians, and Brigadier General in the service of the United States, do solemnly swear to bear true allegiance to the said United States of America, And to serve them honestly and faithfully against all their enemies or opposers whomsoever, and to observe and Obey the orders of the President of the United States of America, And the Orders of the officers appointed Over me, According to the articles of war, and the true intent and meaning of the secret articles of the treaty of peace, made and concluded between the united States of America, and the Creek nation of Indians, On the seventh day of the Present month of August

Alex: McGillivray

Sworn before me in the City of New York This Fourteenth day of August in the year of our Lord One thousand Seven hundred and Ninety.

John Blair an associate judge of the supreme Court of the United States —

ALEXANDER MCGILLIVRAY'S 1790 OATH OF ALLEGIANCE
TO THE UNITED STATES GOVERNMENT

MENAWA, THE RED STICK CREEK WHO LED
THE ATTACK ON FORT MIMS, ALABAMA, IN 1813

in a better position to keep their land. George Washington invited McGillivray to the U.S. capital. After his visit, Thomas Jefferson proclaimed that no Indian land should be taken without their consent. Unfortunately, when McGillivray died no one with his diplomatic skill took over. Whites were allowed to take Creek lands, and the Creeks were divided into factions.

Violent earthquakes shook the Southeast in 1811 and 1812. Creek shamans said the quakes were a sign from the Master of Breaths. They told their Red Stick warriors it was time to fight. The warriors, led by Menawa, attacked Fort Mims in Alabama. Sometimes called the Sacred Revolt, the Creek War was also a civil war between Nontraditional Creeks, who lived like white people, and Traditionals, who kept to the old ways. Some Creeks, but mostly whites, lived at Fort Mims. Almost everyone in the fort was killed.

U.S. soldiers led by General Andrew Jackson, along with some Cherokees and Nontraditional Creeks, attacked the Traditionals at Horseshoe Bend, Alabama. Women and children were allowed to leave before the attack, but eight hundred Creek warriors died. Livestock were killed. Corn fields, barns, and

CREEK CHIEF WEATHERFORD SURRENDERS TO ANDREW JACKSON
AFTER THE BATTLE AT HORSESHOE BEND, ALABAMA, IN 1814.

houses were burned. Jackson then forced defeated Creeks to sign a treaty giving up millions of acres of precious territory.

Since the arrival of Europeans, Creeks had traded with the French, Spanish, and English, fought with the English against the Spanish, and remained neutral in the Revolutionary War. The league Creeks tried to form with other southeastern tribes did not last.

THE REMOVAL

Whites kept coming to the Southeast seeking land. Andrew Jackson, elected president in 1828, decided there wasn't enough land for Indians and whites, so Indians had to go. The Indian Removal Act became law in 1830. Creeks, Choctaws, Cherokees, Chickasaws, and Seminoles—called the Five Civilized Tribes because some lived like whites—were forced to sign Treaties of Removal. In these agreements, the government promised to pay for their land in the Southeast and give them land west of the Mississippi River not yet divided into states.

Several hundred Nontraditional Creeks in Georgia, led by Roley McIntosh, traveled to Indian Territory on their own. They had already been paid for their land. Others were allowed to stay in Alabama if they gave up their shared farmland and accepted a small plot for each family. This did not work out,

ROLEY MCINTOSH LED A GROUP OF CREEK TO
INDIAN TERRITORY (NOW OKLAHOMA)
BEFORE THE REMOVAL BEGAN.

because Indians were not allowed to testify against whites in court. If a white person said an Indian owed him money, the Indian couldn't prove he didn't; he had to give the white his land. Some Georgia Traditionals left their homes and went to Alabama when whites took over their land. "Poor, hungry, and ill-clothed," an English traveler wrote, "they wandered about like bees whose hive had been destroyed."

The government warned other members of the Five Tribes that unless they left on their own by a certain date, the U.S. army would force them to go. Creek men sank into despair, for they could no longer protect their homes and families. Some Creeks joined the Seminoles in Florida, because the Seminoles had been given a later deadline. Others isolated themselves in swamps in southern Alabama, near the western border of the Florida panhandle.

Then the final order came. Those who hadn't already left or gone into hiding were forced from their homes. The Choctaws were forced out first. Remaining Creeks followed in 1837 and 1838. They put out the sacred fires in italwa squares, abandoned their homes, gardens, and fields, and began their journey. Through freezing cold and blazing heat, U.S. soldiers herded Creek people west on what became known as the Trail of Tears. Most did not understand why they had to go. Some of the eldest rode in wagons with the smallest children. Most walked, many barefoot, often drenched with rain, as they sloshed through mud or trod over hard, cold ground. Three hundred people drowned when they were packed onto a creaky old boat that sank in the Mississippi River.

The command came suddenly, one Creek woman said. She saw crowded wagons passing her home. Then some stopped and men came in and told her to gather her things. They waited impatiently, but she hardly knew what to take. The men took her and her children to a stockade where others waited. No one spoke, she said. The silence was frightening. Finally, others came and the journey began. Many fell, too weak with hunger to keep up. They were left to die alone on makeshift grass beds.

Another woman, a child when she left, told how her grandfather had died on the way. He was left with only a piece of cottonwood on his body and placed beside a stream. "Someone sang on the wrecked boat," another woman said. "I can't forget the words. 'I have no more land. I am driven away from home, driven up the red waters. Let us all go. Let us die together. Somewhere upon the banks we will be there.'"

FORCED REMOVAL TO INDIAN TERRITORY WAS ESPECIALLY HARD
ON WOMEN AND CHILDREN. THOUSANDS FROM THE CREEK,
CHEROKEE, AND OTHER TRIBES DIED ALONG THE WAY FROM
SICKNESS, STARVATION, OR DROWNING.

INDIAN TERRITORY WAS A HARSHER, MORE RUGGED LAND
THAN THE ONE CREEKS WERE FORCED TO LEAVE.

No one knows how many died of sickness, starvation, exposure, or drowning. An estimated fifty thousand people were "removed" on that shameful journey.

Creek troubles weren't over when they arrived in Indian Territory. More people died of sickness or starvation. The government promised to provide food, but it came late and was of poor quality. Meat was old. Grain had weevils. In the Southeast, winters were mild, summers long and moist. To the west, however, winters were colder, and it snowed. Summers were hot, and hail fell, sometimes as big as stones. Even worse, violent tornadoes blew homes away.

The Nontraditionals had settled on the eastern part of land assigned to the Creek, and old hostilities flared. Nontraditionals looked down on Traditionals, calling them ignorant. Nontraditionals and many whites thought all Indians should *assimilate*— become Christians, speak English, and work, farm, and live like whites. Traditionals wanted to practice their own faith, speak their own language, and farm as they always had, on land shared with clan members and neighbors. They settled on the western part of Creek territory to avoid conflict.

Equipment for farming and construction promised by the government also came late. The

Creeks cleared the land with the few tools they had brought. They planted corn and vegetables and built temporary shelters covered with animal skins or tree bark. In time they built log cabins. Successful Creek built larger homes, grew cotton, and even owned slaves like white southerners. They laid out their towns like those in the east and gave them the same names. Money the government paid for Creeks' eastern land was spent on schools, and missionaries came to teach, preach, and build churches.

Trouble arose when members of other tribes raided Creek settlements. In 1842 the Creeks called for a council meeting. Delegates from eighteen tribes met, including Cherokees, Chickasaws, Seminoles, Osages, and broken bands driven from the east. They exchanged ideas about defending themselves and planned to help each other catch and punish criminals. The tribes condemned liquor and pledged not to give or sell land without consulting with the other tribes.

In 1861, during the U.S. Civil War, Chocktaws, Chickasaws, and Seminoles met with Creeks and formed the United Nations of Indian Territory to decide what position to take. Nontraditional Creeks sided with the South. Even though Opothle Yoholo, who now led the Traditionals, owned slaves, he urged

THE LOG CABINS THAT THE CREEKS BUILT FOR THEMSELVES IN
INDIAN TERRITORY WERE MORE SUITED TO THE FRONTIER
ENVIRONMENT THAN THEIR HOMES IN THE SOUTHEAST.

IN 1875 DELEGATES FROM THIRTY TRIBES MET AT THE
CREEK COUNCIL HOUSE TO DISCUSS THE PROBLEMS
THEY HAD IN COMMON.

all Indians not to take sides. It was a white man's war, he said. Indians should not become involved.

When southern soldiers overran Creek territory, Yoholo led several thousand Creeks north to Kansas. Southern soldiers attacked them on the way. Creeks lost wagons, livestock, and everything else they had with them. At war's end, survivors returned to Indian Territory after soldiers destroyed their homes, schools, and livestock. Then the U.S. government refused to distinguish between Creeks who sided with the Confederacy and those who sided with the Union. All Creeks were treated as enemies and forced to sell much of their land for very little money.

In 1867 representatives of both Creek groups, working together, wrote a constitution for the new Creek Nation. The government was organized some-what like that of the United States. An election was held, and Samuel Checote, a Creek Methodist minis-ter who had been a Confederate army officer, became Principal Chief. Again, Traditionals and Nontraditionals disagreed. Traditionals did not like the new system. It was "white man's way," they said. Arguments and fights broke out for almost twenty years. In 1883 the two groups finally agreed to abide by the new Creek constitution. After all they had been through, they dared to face the future with optimism.

The Creeks' hopefulness would not last long. Four years after the formation of the Creek Nation, the U.S. Congress passed laws that did away with all tribal governments. The laws also forced Creek and other tribes in Indian Territory to give up their shared lands and accept a small plot for each family. Some Creeks accepted an *allotment*. Most refused. They still thought their old system of sharing land was best.

In 1900 Chitto Harjo and his followers set up a Traditional government in the town of Hickory Ground and declared allotment illegal. U.S. soldiers raided their meeting place, and a hundred Creek men were arrested. Unless they accepted allotment, Harjo and his followers faced a long jail term. Some accepted a small plot of land to avoid jail. Only 10 percent of all Creeks accepted small lots. Even though the treaty had promised them the western land for "as long as grass shall grow and rivers run," many leftover acres were sold to white settlers.

Before long, whites wanted Oklahoma Territory, just west of Indian Territory, to become a state. The Creeks and other tribes in Indian Territory wished to remain independent. Representatives of the Five Civilized Tribes wrote a constitution for an Indian state. They called it Sequoyah, after the man who

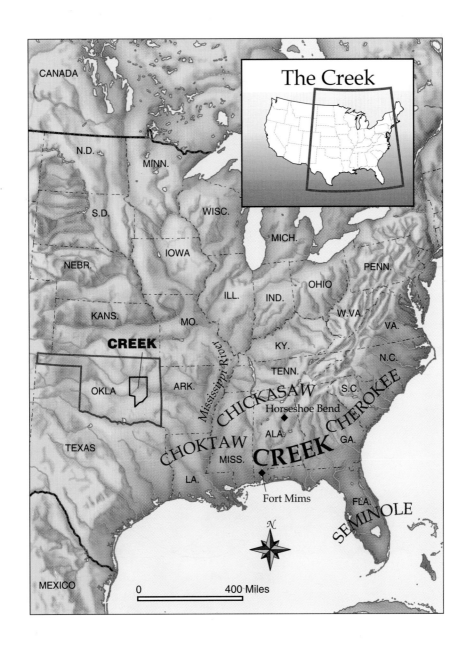

The Creek

CANADA

N.D.

MINN.

S.D.

WISC.

MICH.

NEBR.

IOWA

PENN.

OHIO

ILL.

IND.

W.VA.

VA.

KANS.

MO.

KY.

CREEK

TENN.

N.C.

OKLA

ARK.

CHICKASAW

S.C.

CHEROKEE

Horseshoe Bend

TEXAS

CHOKTAW

MISS.

ALA.

CREEK

GA.

LA.

Fort Mims

FLA.

SEMINOLE

MEXICO

Mississippi River

N

0   400 Miles

SOME CREEKS BECAME WEALTHY WHEN OIL WAS
FOUND ON THEIR PROPERTY IN THE EARLY 1900s,
BUT MOST REMAINED POOR.

invented a Cherokee system of writing. The constitution was sent to Washington, D.C., and ignored. In 1907 Indian Territory and Oklahoma Territory—combined—became the state of Oklahoma.

When oil was discovered near the Creek town of Tulsa, the state appointed guardians to help Creek people manage the large amounts of money oil companies paid to rent their land. Some of the guardians collected the Creeks' money and kept it for themselves. Even money that some Creek children were supposed to get because of their parents' deaths was taken by the guardians.

The stock market crash in 1929 and the Great Depression that followed caused many people in the United States, including Creeks, to lose their jobs. Franklin D. Roosevelt, who became president in 1932, believed government should help needy people. Tribal governments were reorganized, the allotment system was discontinued, and the U.S. government supplied the Creek Nation with funds to buy back some of its land. The Creek capital complex was established, and the Creeks built businesses, housing, and health care centers.

LIFE TODAY

"Remember," writes the poet Joy Harjo of the Tiger Clan. Her great-great-grandfather was Menawa, the famous Red Stick warrior who survived the Creek War but probably died on the Trail of Tears. Much of Joy Harjo's poetry stresses the importance of Creek history.

Most of the two thousand members of the Poarch Creek Band in Alabama cannot remember their clan names, because they have been separated from their relatives for so long. The Poarch are descendants of Creek who escaped forced removal from the Southeast by hiding in the foggy, snake-infested swamps of southern Alabama. Now they often meet with descendants of the other Five Tribes who avoided removal and are scattered throughout the Southeast. On the Poarch reservation near the town of Atmore, they participate in traditional celebrations and historical programs.

Today, Creeks in eastern Oklahoma and in Alabama own farms and businesses, have jobs, and live much like whites. Creeks are also lawyers, doctors, teachers, and other

MANY CREEK IN OKLAHOMA TODAY HOLD PROFESSIONAL
JOBS, SUCH AS THIS PHYSICIAN'S ASSISTANT.

JOY HARJO, CREEK POET, MUSICIAN, AND
GREAT-GREAT-GRANDDAUGHTER OF THE RED STICK
WARRIOR MENAWA

professionals. Profits from high-stakes bingo parlors operated by the Creek Nation of Oklahoma help support a health center and hospital, which are staffed by Indian doctors and nurses. Bingo operations also provide college money, programs for the elderly, and cultural activities for youth.

For many years the U.S. president appointed the Creeks' Principal Chief. In 1971 Congress voted that Creeks could once again elect their own chief. Claude Cox held the post for many years. He fought for and won federally funded health care programs, educational and employment programs, low-cost housing, and aid for farmers. Perry Beaver was elected Principal Chief in 1995. When he was sworn in he said, "The Muscogee Nation will not give up any more of our sovereignty." His statement reflects a desire many Creeks have to restore and preserve many of the traditional elements of their culture.

Although more and more Creeks have married non-Indians through the years, many continue to identify with their clans. Some of the differences between Traditionals and Nontraditionals, differences that split the tribe when European culture influenced them, are still there. But as with other tribes, there is a revival of interest in "roots," or early culture. A Creek Heritage Museum has been established in the capital at Okmulgee.

Poskita, the Green Corn Ceremony, is still the most important celebration of the year. It links people of the past

CREEKS DANCING IN A CIRCLE AS
THEIR ANCESTORS DID

with those of the present and future. Some church services in Oklahoma towns are held in the Creek language. The Creek language is also taught in schools in several towns. Some students use computers to go on the Internet and write to "pen pals" about the Creek Indian culture. Children are learning what their ancestors' tribes were called before whites called them all Creeks. "I am Hitchiti Muscogee and a member of the Raccoon Clan," one says. Another says, "I am Coweta Creek of the Bear Clan."

Students from the Eufaula Creek Nation Boarding School perform an annual dance dramatizing the forced removal of the Five Civilized Tribes from their eastern homeland. "Remember," Joy Harjo wrote. By remembering how Creek culture has survived through difficult times, its tradition lives on.

GLOSSARY

Allotment U.S. Government's 1887 policy dividing tribal land into small plots to be owned by one person or family. Allotment is also the word for one of the plots.

Assimilate To become absorbed into the culture of another group of people.

Breechcloth A cloth or animal skin that hangs from a belt around the waist.

Chakofa Building in which Creek held winter councils.

Clan Group of people belonging to the same family.

Conquistadors Spanish explorers who overran native peoples in the Americas in the sixteenth century.

Herbalists People who collect and learn to use plants as medicine.

Italwa Muscogee word for town.

Mico Muscogee word for chief.

Midwives Women who help other women in childbirth.

Plantation A large farm or estate cultivated by workers or slaves who live on it.

Poskita Creek word for Green Corn Festival.

Red Stick Muscogee (or Creek) warrior. They were called Red Stick because their totems, or poles, were painted red.

Shaman A priest who uses magic to cure the sick and foresee the future.

Sofky Traditional soup made from corn ground into cornmeal.

Spanish moss A stringy plant that hangs from trees in the southern United States.

Taboo Forbidden.

Totem An animal or plant considered related to a clan and used as a symbol. A totem pole is a stick that is decorated to represent the clan.

FOR FURTHER READING

Bruchac, Joseph. *The Great Ball Game: A Muskogee Story.* Illustrated by Susan L. Roth. New York: Dial, 1994.

Fremon, David. *The Trail of Tears.* New York: Macmillan, 1994.

Green, Michael D. *The Creeks.* New York: Chelsea House, 1990.

Lee, Martin. *The Seminoles.* New York: Franklin Watts, 1989.

Maestro, Betsy and Giulio. *Exploration and Conquest: The Americas After Columbus, 1500–1620.* New York: Lothrop, 1994.

Wallin, Luke. *In the Shadow of the Wind.* New York: Bradbury Press, 1984.

INDEX

ABOUT THE AUTHOR

Shirlee P. Newman has written fifteen books for children, including two others in the Franklin Watts Indians of the Americas series: *The Incas* and *The Inuits.* Her books include biographies, fiction, folk tales, and a picture book, and she has worked as Associate Editor at *Child Life Magazine.* She has published articles and stories in several other magazines. She lives in Massachusetts.